I remember

I remember

a communal memory of the pandemic
composed for Scotland's Covid Memorial

alec finlay

Stewed Rhubarb
2022

The concept of *'I remember'* was devised by Joe Brainard, who published his own collection in 1975. It has since been adopted, with gratitude, by a number of artists and writers.

*'I remember'*, copyright of the Joe Brainard estate, © 1975, 2022

In 2020 The Herald established a public fund to create Scotland's Covid Memorial; the artwork in Pollok Country Park is accompanied by an audiobook, website, and this publication.

*for the dead and those still finding
their way to healing*

I remember

I remember
how our evening
walk became
a strange walk

I remember
driving to
Barnard Castle
to test my eyes

I remember
learning to
read eyes
amid the loss
of lips

I remember
that first summer —
the garden never
looked better

I remember
my wee boy's
laughter as he
played tag with
the other children
on the playground—
I hope he remembers
it too

I remember
all those
sourdough
starters

I remember finding sanctuary and solace swimming at the bend of the river

I remember
a smattering of snow
& Ava counting up
to ten

I remember plotting to coincidentally bump into Mam in the garden centre, and crying by the roses

I remember
my hands shaking
as I withdrew the
first covid vaccine
to administer to the
oldest patient in our
practice, and tears
in my eyes as I
administered it

I remember
when we could see
people again - everyone
looked so beautiful

I remember
realising I was
not getting better

I remember
the bus-stop was
out of reach

I remember
learning to be
gentler with
myself

I remember
how, without the comforts
and the pace of my
pre-covid life, my deep
interests were all
that was left of me,
like quiet embers
that have lasted
in an otherwise
consuming darkness

I remember
not being afraid
to hug my
patients !!!

I remember coming home after shifts and crying in the doorway unable to hug anyone until I was clean

I remember
wishing I could
cut open
my rib-cage

I remember
being ill and
the serenity
in the breath-
lessness

I remember when my mum could remember our names

I remember
her standing
by the fallen tree
and saying
that's me,
I'm broken

I remember
grandad said that
in past wars familes
had tied yellow ribbons
around trees in
remembrance of
the men who left,
and so we made
a yellow heart

I remember
Mum, Margaret,
She loved us all,
Shoes and shopping
xx

I remember Andrea

I remember
Big Eileen
She was a
pure tonic

I remember how 2019 changed our lives

I remember sunset when nothing was amiss

I remember being sick in February and everyone telling me it
    wasn't Covid

I remember Valentine's Day 2020, in the beauty salon: the radio
    said the mayor of Milan had locked down the city – it was
    then I knew I had to isolate immediately

I remember taking panic attacks going to the supermarket even
    before lockdown, due to watching events in China

I remember how scared I was

I remember receiving an email telling me to prepare for the worst
    and hope for the best

I remember the magnified importance of those events that took
    place in the weeks just before lockdown

I remember when nobody had died

I remember walking amongst ancient graves, reading their stories
    and thinking my generation was lucky to have missed plagues
    and war, but now our turn had come


I remember our ultra-religious neighbour started wearing his
    *the rapture is coming* t-shirt


I remember seeing the empty toilet roll shelves at Tesco on Holy
    Corner and buying a pack in Tain


I remember Covid jokes and comical videos – they stopped abruptly
    when reality hit home, it wasn't funny anymore


I remember choking with pity at the sight of the bats and pangolins
    in a wet market in China


I remember my disbelief in the slowness of our government to act
    and fearing the consequences would span years and impact
    millions of lives


I remember when they stopped testing


I remember the advice not to wear a mask


I remember I was like a kettle, I was boiling

I remember the fear of the unknown, aware we were encountering
    a challenge we had never experienced before

I remember walking with my younger son on the first day
    of lockdown and we wondered what a lockdown might be

I remember, at the very start of lockdown, an extraordinarily sunny
    day looking out of my bay window onto the deserted silent city

I remember watching *'Normal People'*, alone, in bed, fevered,
    not sure if I'd live – the characters felt like the last friends
    I'd spend time with

I remember writing a farewell letter to my family, *"just in case"*,
    and being surprised by how much happiness I recalled

I remember the compassion in the solicitor's voice when
    I updated my will in a rush

I remember my daughter's anxiety and how we agreed not
    to watch the news

I remember the world stopped when the Prime Minister said
    on TV *"You Must Stay At Home"*

I remember feeling so helpless

I remember when the worst-case scenario was 20,000 deaths

I remember not celebrating but singing 'Happy Birthday' to myself
    while washing hands

I remember *'Hands, Face, Space'*

I remember learning a brand-new language – *'shielding', 'proning',*
    *'zoom bombing', 'lockdown easing'*

I remember regular briefings from smiling politicians with
    careful eyes

I remember slogans, chaos – *'stay at home',* then *'stay alert'* –
    & struggling to make sense

I remember Boris bumbling, blowing bubbles, telling us:
    *'get out & shop'*

I remember Nicola's ability to channel disapproval, and Boris'
    nod and a wink

I remember him saying that the only difference between Nicola
    and Boris was *'a comb and an iron'*


I remember thinking the Queen talked a lot more sense than
    Boris Johnson


Is cuimhin liom an domhan go léir faoi cheilt
(I remember the whole world in purdah)


I remember flights carrying on as normal, and no checks at airports


I remember my daughter walking an hour to and from work to
    prevent further losses in the Care Home


I remember a new etiquette when passing folk on the path


I remember that in the first week of lockdown I parked in an empty
    car park and someone took the time to leave me a laminated
    A3 note telling me not to park there again


I remember doors being slowly opened, light spilling out into the
    dark, the sound of metal pans being beaten, carrying through
    the cold air that first night of clapping

I remember listening to the rain as if I'd never heard it before

I remember the kids in our street leaving me a chalk written message surrounded by a heart

I remember folk making masks, then hanging them from trees, like ripe fruit for us to pick

I remember being fearful for the future of the children in my class as they walked across the playground on the last day of school before lockdown – how many of their young lives would emerge unscathed from the pandemic?

I remember Kai asking if we could have a sleepover after the germs have gone

I remember my doctor wishing me luck as she told me there was nothing they could do for me

I remember Mum being handed her meds through a cunning side window in her GP surgery

I remember my daughter's arrival home after her long journey from London to be with me during the first lockdown – she was wearing blue surgical gloves and said she hadn't touched her face once throughout the journey

I remember not wanting to be alone but god those around me
    are too noisy


I remember feeling overwhelmed trying to home-school our kids
    and work alongside them; how it tested then strengthened
    our family relationships – Monday mornings were the worst,
    so we baked and went outdoors


I remember my son phoning me every single night on a video chat,
    sometimes only for two or three minutes, for all the months
    of lockdown, when we couldn't see each other face to face –
    it made all the difference


I remember my beautiful girls trying to help me get through it
    and their different ways of looking after me


I remember feeling like I was expendable because I'm disabled


I remember being told to clap for the NHS, as though that was
    going to pay a nurse's bills, put food on their table, or provide
    adequate PPE


I remember how awful it was because we 'deaf' people have been cut
    off from the world, and not communicating due to technology
    teething problems – thankful for Interpreter Now (trained BSL)
    who set that platform for us to communicate with the outside
    isolated world

I remember when the cry was: *'you're on mute!'*


I remember how you all turned up with such loving kindness
    and stayed


I remember everyone outdoors gardening loudly whilst I was
    indoors going quietly insane


I remember working from home yet living at work


I remember the world was the same, but more awkwardly made


I remember wonky avocados


I remember washing the shopping


I remember the chap at the door for a parcel


I remember the masked drivers delivering groceries, who never
    failed to ask how are you?


I remember the queue outside Tesco at 9 o'clock on a sun-crisp
    Wednesday morning: we're here because it's Old Gits Hour

I remember craving bananas when the shelves were bare

I remember my mum said she just missed going to the supermarket

I remember sterilising & scouring with surgical spirits, soap & water, tea tree & lavender

I remember two men in high viz, arms measuring the distance between their mouths

I remember how I smiled when I received a single toilet roll in the post from a friend in Wales

I remember mountain goats invading Llandudno

I remember the first day of shielding, being in a room on my own with a TV and my daughter bringing me food

I remember all the people who have been careful and how it's helped

I remember a socially-distanced conga at the supermarket

I remember I was scouring the already ransacked aisles of ASDA when you called, after weeks of illness, and realising it might be the last time we ever spoke

I remember the self-service check out in Morrisons saying it only accepted card payments and asking, *'Do you wish to continue?'* and thinking there we have a question that gets to the heart of things

I remember you at nine months old, sat amongst the sacks of lentils and towers of Fray Bentos pies, playing peekaboo with PPE and chewing on a cardboard box – an un-sanitisable parcel square in the middle of the food bank floor, pointing the way out of this pandemic through care and fellow feeling, as long in this world as in the womb and already learning fast just what is to be done

I remember your orchids on our windowsill couldn't care less about quarantine

I remember the flicker of buds on ivy-clad trees

I remember sitting in the park alone listening to the comforting sound of a creaking tree

I remember Covidly walking in April, skylarks and snow showers on the moor

I remember us marching on in the stotting rain, unperturbed,
    refreshed by something different


I remember when I watched the barnacles closely enough to see
    them open in the tide, and then realised that the rocks beneath
    my feet were alive


I remember a cobbled lane and me beneath blossom and a
    blackbird's song, as the sun dripped, draped shadows
    by my feet


I remember my first 'walk' in the wheelchair, meeting Annie,
    and we agreed the wild garlic seems early every year


I remember an acrobatic squirrel tumbling his wilkies, showing
    off to no-one in particular, or was it for me?


I remember sitting in my two-square-metres of potted solitude,
    baking under the sun


I remember her telling me that, though she can't go out now, every
    day she imagines a walk, pausing at each bench to take in the
    view from memory


I remember faces looking out of their house windows watching
    the world go by

I remember hoarding time for after it's all over


I remember walking every day to nowheres, dreaming of
    somewheres I'd already been


I remember longing for places I may never visit and places
    I once knew


I remember that I travelled the world during lockdown, on trains,
    planes, boats, thanks to TV and dreams


I remember tying dandelion flowers around my big toe


I remember creating a wildlife pond and the joy of watching
    my first tadpoles emerge


I remember the first lockdown – space to slow down, time to reflect,
    and to fix the shed, re-felted at last in the sunshine


I remember Marvin Gaye asking 'What's Goin' On' from a Glasgow
    street window


I remember a white man's knee on a black man's throat, while so
    many tried to breathe with Covid

I remember banging pots with wooden spoons while opposite
    a sax played 'Somewhere Over The Rainbow'


I remember feeling upbeat while others mourned a loss of freedom
    – my being used to the loss


I remember life going on as normal in the first lockdown because
    I've worked from home for years!


I remember being grasped in the grip of aspic time, wrapped too
    tight in this shrunken life


I remember a magic time, a topsy-turvy time, when past, present,
    future intertwined & all there was was now


I remember 4am, awake, fretting and thinking I might as well
    squeeze some work in before the home school day


I remember Joe Wicks


I remember when Alexa became my daily and only companion


I remember Captain Tom Moore

I remember walking around the garden trying to keep fit

I remember ambulance sirens streaming through the screen during yoga Zooms, and after clicking *'leave'*, the uncanny quiet of the glen

I remember that first lockdown contentedness, living like a peasant in the eighteenth century, digging the soil, not straying, staying local, finding new paths

I remember our allotment neighbour Bill hadn't been digging his plot, eventually his wife told us he was in the Royal in a coma on a ventilator – before that he'd been training to run a marathon

I remember growing French beans for the first time

I remember learning how to bake

I remember fire-pits & hearths & candles & stories under stars & unexpected gifts

I remember children suckling on iPads

I remember friendships now faint as a sickle moon, and others sweetly blooming, ruffled by the breeze on Zoom

I remember notes tied to door-knobs & gifts left on the mat when
    Covid kept us far apart


I remember no hugging, kissing, shaking of hands, just waving from
    across the street


I remember reclusiveness was normalised


I remember how I learnt to live with the windows wide open


I remember my granddaughter living alone in a high rise flat,
    seeing no one and not able to get out


I remember signs prohibiting entry to parks and playgrounds


I remember the unusual yet suddenly natural feeling of finally being
    in tune with a locked down society; like my introvert inclination
    finally found equilibrium with the outside world


I remember the shock that followed losing my job, a week before
    the furlough scheme was announced – 150 colleagues were
    also affected


I remember the haunting quietness of my daily journey

I remember running along Princes St when there were no people and no cars


I remember Bootcamp on the empty Meadows with my son


I remember the lines in the centre of the road – if I walked along them I was far enough away from passers-by on either side, but close enough to say hello


I remember travelling to work on an eerily quiet motorway, longing for the normality of a traffic jam


I remember realising no one had ever seen what I could see: the Royal Mile totally empty on a sunny Saturday afternoon


I remember walking down Belmont St as I had done most days for the past 50 years and hearing a pleasantly cheerful gurgling sound, then realising it was the River Kelvin deep in its gorge unfettered from the roar of traffic


I remember my shoes, at the door, sulking, scowling


I remember seven months in – an abundance of geraniums & a pile of worn-out boots

I remember time slipping through fingers, landing in heaps around
	my feet, disappearing


I remember four weeks into lockdown thinking *'it must almost
	be over by now'*


I remember a no-clock, snap-shot, feet-up, fed-up time


I remember time thickening like porridge in the pot


I remember life, like a ship, slipping past my window – a mere
	smear, here, there, gone


I remember a small dog with a yellow scarf which read *'nervous'*


I remember a wooden seat, hazard-warning wrapped in red and
	white, yellow NHS message: *'never use these benches'*


I remember weekly litter picking masks from the gutters in
	Garrioch Road


I remember myself and the bus driver on an empty bus – shared fear in
	our eyes – the driver called it the 'Covid run', because I worked in the
	local hospital, then he cracked a joke and offered to take a diversion
	to Largs, and we temporarily forgot about the empty streets

I remember making eye contact with a white cat nonchalantly licking
    itself in the middle of the normally busy road, not a car in sight,
    while I furtively scuttled by on my illicit 3rd walk of the day


I remember my friend soaking his feet every morning in warm
    water to ease the pain


I remember Kate arranging fresh air haircuts in her garden


I remember cutting my mum's hair and her complaining, and
    having to wait until she was asleep so I could finish it


I remember being inside, cocooned, while outside life moved on


I remember having time to stand and stare and marvel


I remember in the stillness and silence we let nature flourish
    and grow


I remember when the cars stopped, and the sound of birdsong
    became so loud that I felt giddy


I remember the eerie beauty of silent roads, silent playgrounds,
    skies filled with ghost birds

I remember birds in the huff & sky smeared with bitter clouds
    which skittered, skited, skelped

I remember silent buses sliding past like hearses

I remember the Super Moon on a day of rising deaths, the wee
    sma hours lit by a golden light

I remember how much it meant to me to see the sleepless swifts
    on the wing out of my evening window

I remember the tight sky, stretched from east to west, over Orkney's
    respectful hush

I remember my lockdown 50th – just a swim in the sea, the full
    moon my guest

I remember on my birthday, realising family and friends had
    my back – then I collapsed

I remember desperately wanting to be alone, in a house full
    of noise, and thinking about all the people out there alone
    and not wanting to be

I remember raising a glass at the Tipsy Angel, an imaginary Zoom bar

I remember the thrill of zooming into theatres, galleries, museums
    and poets' front rooms

I remember playing so many games of Scrabble that I could
    go on 'Countdown'

I remember cancelling our wedding – we held an unofficial
    ceremony instead, just us two and the dogs

I remember going to church 'on telly'

I remember meeting my colleague at the crematorium one Spring
    sunrise – him pointing out the deer grazing, and introducing
    me to the squirrels that he knew by name – and it feeling like
    a privilege for us to have the grounds to ourselves at that hour,
    and a privilege to be able to help people when they needed us

I remember a riverside walk, the river still flowing, still doing
    what rivers do

I remember when we got excited looking at what we thought
    was a kingfisher – it was only a blue bag

I remember loving the peace of the riverside, then the jolt
    of realising the loss of life that the peace had cost

I remember finding sanctuary and solace swimming at the bend in the river

I remember wild-swimmers on the beach, the women emerging from their chrysalis changing robes

I remember the early mornings lying in the garden at daybreak to get any cool air

I remember it was so quiet on the road – I could hear more birds, and then came the walkers and their dogs, and eventually the mothers and fathers carrying babies born during quarantine

I remember when we went to look for the Primula scotica

I remember the Blue Mountains – a lost continent inside me

I remember turn-back-over, snuggle-back-down days, when everything and everyone seemed grey

I remember on our daily walk the prom was dotted with small family groups, everyone looking out over the Clyde and asking if the sky had ever been so dazzlingly, breathtakingly clear, bright and blue before

I remember the low lands, the low hills rolling, just a wee bit north of local civilization, few trees, not far from the coast, presage of the high lands somehow; looking out over low lands with no human figures there for now, low, loch, down


I remember a community hall where hearts and voices were raised, and a great tree was hung with lights that glowed bright and lovely through the long dark


I remember season tumbling into season – sirens, distance, birdsong, zoom


I remember the radio spurting Covid news and scientific views, while time flew by like autumn geese


I remember watching squirrels fatten, wood pigeons woo, blue tits flit & winter trees shed autumn's gold


I remember watching from my kitchen window as the sun set between two ash trees


I remember the acers on fire & apples begging me 'pick'


I remember a robin coming right to the edge of the path to the closest twig and singing there – as if I was Snow White!

I remember a pink-cheeked boy dragging a disappointed sledge through snow-melt sludge

I remember winter went on so long, I thought I would die of loneliness

I remember mislaid Covid masks scattered like leaves on post-ice gravelled pavements

I remember stepping out to find the light on Solstice

I remember Christmas Eve & presents on my doorstep

I remember the last of the first snowdrops

I remember us filling the hollow in our conversation with what we'd eaten that day – there wasn't much else to say

I remember Mum, eating every meal alone at her kitchen table, for months on end

I remember my elderly parents becoming condensed into a bubble on the end of a telephone

I remember the daily statistics and weeping for people I didn't know

I remember how – perhaps because the days were becalmed –
    we became more aware than ever of the fins of sadness,
    illness and pain that circle us and those we love; moving
    in and away, in and away


I remember you didn't look back at me when I walked away


I remember the comfort of the radio when I was ill and alone


I remember the heart-pain when my 13-year old daughter wouldn't
    get out of bed, open the curtains, and what a dark place the
    pandemic could be for some people


I remember spending lockdown with my new-born baby and
    bonding with him, with no interruptions or outside pressures


I remember crying about the effect that lockdown had on the
    mental health of my 16-year old niece


I remember lockdown unlocking my daughter's imagination
    and creativity – this slower life helped expand her mind
    and vocabulary in ways nursery and our societal need for
    'education' never managed to


I remember a footballer ensuring all the kids got a daily meal

I remember the day I returned to work after first lockdown
    started, my wide-eyed, beautifully innocent, 5-year old
    daughter, reflecting my own anxiety, saying *'I'm scared
    Mummy'*, to which I replied *'I am scared too sweet heart,
    but sometimes even when we are scared we have to just
    get on and do the right thing'*


I remember standing in the dark in my garden at 3am during the
    first lockdown and, for the first time, not hearing the constant
    traffic noise, instead being deafened by the sound of birdsong –
    it made me cry and filled me with hope


I remember the basket of gifts they brought – chaga, fresh sage,
    tender broccoli, turmeric, and a perfect pomegranate


I remember microdosing


I remember being appalled by all the anti-vaxxers on Tinder


I remember socially distanced pubs like gap-toothed OAPs


I remember bedlam at the bar, replaced by table service, order,
    decorum, more civilised by far


I remember tears of relief streaming as the news broke –
    the vaccine rollout had commenced

I remember being excited when I went for my first vaccine
    to be participating in something enormous


I remember the lack of distinction made between those who won't
    take the vaccine, and those that can't


I remember trying to assemble the box for my first Covid test kit


I remember the rule of six


I remember hearing the army were coming to keep us in our homes


I remember when the daily death toll was more than the Titanic


I remember the PM thought the first lockdown was a mistake


I remember the third lockdown, becoming unusually insular,
    trepidatious, not wanting to be elsewhere


I remember my South African cousin told me 17 members of her
    immediate community, both friends and colleagues, were dead
    from Covid, and feeling guilty because I'd had two vaccine jabs
    and my colleagues and friends were still healthy

I remember realising the extent to which our genetic inheritance
    shapes our lives and our immune systems determine our fate


I remember you in bed for a whole month – that was over a year
    ago; still you can only taste citrus, only smell the strange
    sweetness of dead mice


I remember Covid turned my piss sour


I remember bed as a magnet, resistance futile


I remember the brick wall that marked the end of my 150-metre
    walk (and world)


I remember when I could walk for miles and didn't, and now I wish
    that I had


I remember how, each day, I tried to go two yards more, but couldn't
    without relapsing


I remember the last walk I was able to take


I remember the bathroom floor when I couldn't leave it for five days

I remember the trauma of trying to eat one bite of toast

I remember the carpet as I lay flat, trying to gasp my way through a bout of air hunger

I remember being left by the wayside

I remember he felt that, after months of illness, his child had abandoned hope

I remember believing I'd get better

I remember the words *'Long Covid'*, spoken out loud, and how much worse than *'Covid Positive'* that was

I remember the realisation that I was in my thirties and might never be well enough to work as a doctor again

I remember not speaking for a few days so that I would be able to speak clearly on a call with the doctor and her writing *'not breathless'* on my notes

I remember people were told they had to exercise, when what they needed was rest

I remember doctors dismissing Long-Covid as 'all in the mind' and thinking I've been here before

I remember him saying: *'the only thing that will give me my life back is medical treatment'*

I remember the virus broke her – and how the neurologist said *'just pinch yourself and you'll be fine'*

I remember she couldn't remember the word for radiator

I remember us helping one another to order horse medicine illegally

I remember the doctor saying, *'don't do Boom & Bust! – Plan, Pace, Prioritise'*, that's the alliteration for me

I remember talking about immune systems and lactic acid on Wardie Beach

I remember the support of my colleagues, so kind it made me cry

I remember when I talked to my body, told her that she's capable, and thanked her for what she's been able to do over the last seven months

I remember when small victories meant so much – I would give
    back every one of my medals to be free of this


I remember how the pandemic brought me, kicking and screaming
    – a lot of screaming – back to the path that was meant for me


I remember her saying that, living in the shadow of death, she'd
    come to accept it wasn't the worst thing that could happen


I remember that I always found ageing to be such an elegant
    process, but with Long Covid we're on the far side of the moon,
    beyond the curvature of light


I remember telling those with chronic illness that they had to
    accept some friends would wait with them, but most would
    go on without them


I remember the DWA rejected my GPs letter describing Long
    Covid because, they said, it was based on information that
    came from me


I remember the British government said they'd *'broken the chain
    of transmission'* on a day 1 in 11 people had Covid


I remember being told I would be fine and just not getting better

I remember being too scared to go to sleep because I didn't think I would wake up

I remember feeling reassured whenever I heard a train go by

I remember she was so ill that all her house plants died

I remember the virus sans test results and how my vivid fever dreams drew no lines

I remember days laying in a hospital bed staring out of a window wishing that visitors were allowed

I remember remembering Edwin Muir and half listening out for the strange horses

I remember the exhaustion of sleep deprivation in my hospital bed from endless alarms nearby

I remember the muffled tones from the make-shift office and, in my mind's eye, visualising the gold and silver nomenclature of these meetings – contrasting with the ashen, hypoxia skin that emerged

I remember the emergency alert noise ringing simultaneously from hundreds of cell phones in the grocery store parking lot, while helicopters lifted off the roof of the children's hospital next door

I remember at 3 o'clock in the afternoon I felt dizzy and went to bed, and dreamt people could see into the future, simply by wearing a medical mask over their eyes

I remember the heart panic I felt when my pregnant daughter caught Covid for the third time

I remember the sound of my daughter's voice through the door trying to help me stay

I remember the texture of the paint on the wall as I lay on one side trying to breathe

I remember the triage nurse telling me to die at home instead of hospital

I remember my fear of going into the Covid room that first morning, and doing it anyway with courage and dignity, head held high

I remember my first time seeing a sea of mandatory face masks and feeling overwhelmed, like I was in a dystopian world

I remember my surprise and amusement when I found it easier to
    speak frankly with my gynaecologist when I was hiding behind
    a face mask


I remember caring for patients and speaking with colleagues, with
    masks and visors obscuring my face and muffling my voice, and
    trying to make my eyes speak


I remember tear-soaked masks that sat below desperate eyes


I remember the fear of being a radiotherapy patient with no masks
    available – it felt just a matter of time


I remember my heart breaking every time we had another death


I remember asking, *'what's brought you to the hospital today?'*,
    I remember her blink, *'do you know where you are just now?'*,
    her mouth moved wordlessly, *'can you hear me?'* – I twigged:
    she'd forgotten her hearing aid, me in full regalia: mask,
    helmet visor, gown, gloves, so she couldn't see to lipread
    or hear through fibre and plastic above bleep and whirr
    of monitors – I thought, this is going to be tricky


I remember living in hospital for endless days and I never saw the
    faces of anyone who treated me – they were hidden behind
    masks and I still don't know who they are

I remember cleaning blood and things in the hospital shower, before I cleaned myself

I remember things that I wish I had not seen or had to do

I remember the feeling of absolute fear and despair

I remember a hollow feeling in the hospital – that, on any day, any of us could die

I remember not to say my experience was negative in hospital because it is the British Holy Cow

I remember having to work in the hospital looking after sick patients, but not being allowed to visit my Dad (also a patient) – he's now no longer with us

I remember not being able to visit Jim and hold his hand, tell him he was going to be OK, for the 35 days he was in hospital, and being only able to talk to him via video call for the last 2 weeks of his life

I remember a family's fear and anger as they were forced to take their daughter home to die, rather than leave her in the hospice alone

I remember wondering if it was right to force elderly people to spend what could be their last months on earth in relative isolation

I remember asking if we were doing the right thing and telling my colleagues that this isn't why I became a palliative care nurse

I remember when I started to feel cold and withdrawn, the emotional toll of watching people die alone catching up with me, and ultimately being overwhelmed with anxiety every time I stepped foot inside my beloved workplace

I remember questioning whether I even wanted to be a nurse anymore – how could I be when I felt like I no longer cared at all?

I remember the tears that flowed when my partner reminded me of the things I'd had to deal with while working during a pandemic – he showed me the compassion that I couldn't show myself

I remember feeling so proud of my nursing colleagues

I remember how privileged I felt, being able to go to work as a front-line worker, to make those human connections

I remember the incredible kindness, teamwork and strength among the entire ICU team

I remember the day that four Covid positive patients died on the ward and the nurses were amazing

I remember the clap of honour given to the many volunteers as they filed through the link corridor of the Glasgow Royal Infirmary

I remember starting my career as a midwife in a global pandemic

I remember just wanting to take my baby home and eat macaroni cheese, and wanting my mum, but knowing that she couldn't be there

I remember my partner walking into hospital alone for his kidney transplant, saying goodbye in the car park and crying tears of joy, sadness and worry!

I remember how disappointing my husband was in his inability to care for me at my lowest

I remember all the women who were killed by their partners, and those who experienced domestic abuse, during the pandemic

I remember being lonely, but thankful I was safe from her rages & fists

I remember realising I was going to die in one of the richest nations on earth with the finest healthcare system and that my local hospital and private hospital were empty

I remember the fear we felt when all five of us had Covid, and the sadness and devastation when only four of us survived

I remember talking on the phone to my brother-in-law and him describing how, at the height of his battle with Covid, he did not know what century he was living in

I remember my brother could scarcely stand to pick up his dinner from the doorstep – the thin weak body and gaunt face, home after enduring 10 days in HDU – someone worse needed that hospital bed

I remember unbearable pain, flashing lights, swallowing tubes through my nose, and powerlessness

I remember the putrid acidic smell of disease and long lonely days and nights waiting for death

I remember being triaged out of the hospital care I needed and the long-term effects I will carry for the rest of my life

I remember creating new rituals as a mark of respect: whenever I
 heard an ambulance siren, I would stand and solemnly observe
 the emergency vehicle as it sped along the street below, and
 wish those it contained survival


I remember the fear that I might have killed my family


I remember when I could gather my mother in my arms in the
 garden of the care home


I remember if only I had been called an hour earlier, she would have
 known she was not alone and would have passed in peace, with
 my words of love whispered softly in her ear


I remember saying '*we love you*' through the glass window and
 knowing this was goodbye as you smiled back


I remember she could only see my words written on a little white
 board through the window, while I did my best to hear her
 through the glass – the last time there were only my words
 and deathly silence


I remember the last time she properly heard my voice, in the little
 wooden gazebo in the garden of the care home, finally getting
 some fresh air and out of the box room she had been forced
 to call home

I remember the wonderful care home staff who broke the rules to let us have the most wonderful 101st Birthday Party with my Mother in law and Nana, in March 2020, and then allowed us to spend the last days with her, in May 2020, so she had a family face to see

I remember visiting my learning disabled son in his care home, masked, outdoors, and not being able to hug him

I remember coming back to work, exhausted and relieved and proud

I remember when he went to the graveyard there was a row of new gravestones, and he knew every name

I remember how, when things got tough, Cameron would say *'coorie doon while the doos fly by'*

I remember Isabel's words about returning illness, with love, to the sea – *'she herself the best one to bear it, the great surging sea'*

I remember in the second winter, when a leading scientist said, *'we're nearer the beginning of this than the end'*

I remember trying to get my lover to understand I was categorised as high risk when Omicron scrambled our world

I remember when I stopped hoping I would feel better tomorrow

I remember when the left behind were left behind

I remember when they stopped making staying at home mandatory, as if the virus had stopped being a virus

I remember learning to live with Covid really meant living like Covid no longer exists

I remember when a journalist described people as either frogs or toads in their attitude to Omicron – I wondered, what about all the roadkill hedgehogs?

I remember when Lord Frost said that merry England is the freest country in the world as regards Covid restrictions

I remember a lowering Biblical sunset just as the Omicron variant flooded the country

I remember when they predicted one million infections a week

I remember some said it was mild, while others planned emergency units in hospital car parks

I remember when an expert said that, eventually, we may run out
    of Greek letters


I remember people feeling relieved to have caught Covid again,
    so they no longer had to be afraid of catching it again


I remember the response was too late, too late, each time, too late


I remember when some parties became known as 'gatherings'


I remember the PM addressed the nation wearing a party hat


I remember him saying, with satisfaction, we only bloom once


I remember Old Archie was the first to go, then a second, a third,
    a fourth – I stopped counting


I remember the slight wave the widower made to camera as he left
    the online funeral


I remember feeling so very sad when I heard Joanna's Great Aunt
    had died of Covid after being admitted to hospital for a fall

I remember our last Christmas together as a family of four before
we all contracted Covid, and now there are only two of us left

I remember I said goodbye, told her how much I loved and would
miss her, but she was gone, and my words went unheard

I remember you waving as you went for your Covid test – you never
returned: no conversation, no goodbyes, month on a ventilator,
phone calls, one call, you have gone, I am alone

I remember that dreadful phone-call to say you were not going to
make it – my whole world fell apart

I remember that night as clear as day, the night we got the call

I remember the phone-call outside the hospital to say you had been
taken too soon dad, and my mum's screams of despair

I remember thinking, this cannot be happening, how can I live
without my beloved mum, Eileen: 20th March, 2020, the day
my world changed forever ♥

I remember whimper-whispering *'love you daddy'* and not saying
*'please don't die'*, as a nurse held an iPad to my fading father's ear

I remember my dad Kenny saying *'I don't mind going to my mother'*; he joined her on the 21/04/20


I remember the injustice I felt – that we had stayed away from him for 9 whole months to keep him safe, but he caught Covid and died anyway


I remember when the dreaded, inevitable thing happened and our Grandad died of Covid on Christmas Eve 2020, 9 months after we last saw him


I remember holding David's feet just before he exhaled his last breath


I remember my child who was here and gone under lockdown and I need the world he should have seen to remember him too


I remember Anne, who loved bright colours and bad taste knick-knacks, who faced challenges all her life yet still had the courage and compassion to tell her friends on FaceTime that she was dying


I remember the moment the doctor told me there was no more they could do, my heart felt like it split in two


I remember my baby Calan Sol, his whole life just us under lockdown, making Spring / Summer 2020 the best time of my life

I remember the love she had for her grandchildren, nothing in the
 world mattered more


I remember having to say goodbye to you on a warm summer's day,
 as swallows tended to their young, cupped in their warm nest
 high up in the eaves of the crematorium


I remember swimming in the peat-black water of the Whiteadder
 with her close behind, long-limbed and casting ripples, our
 voices carrying down the river in the evening's dappled
 light – I can return to Whiteadder but not to her


I remember when mum was in hospital for tests and while there
 contracted Covid, RIP


I remember Elizabeth, 1948-2021, always


I remember cooking, walking, chilling out, then I lost you my
 beloved Bob x


I remember you grandma and always will


I remember her friends lining the High Street to wave her goodbye
 because there were too many of them to be allowed to go to
 her funeral

I remember she knew what she was talking about

I remember she was very well spoken

I remember she sounded like a teacher

I remember she was the first to throw a white chrysanthemum

I remember she loved the mallard ducks that live under a bridge, who sleep floating on the stream, or coiled on the grass

I remember she called out for poems in a voice that sang out like the *'sloeblack, slow, black, crowblack, fishingboatbobbing sea'*, of the poet she loved

I remember one of the dear ten who died suddenly at the care home when Skye was hit by a bullet

I remember he dragged each breath from death, each sudden stop, each new breath, until the apple settling in the throat – death found its way

I remember my Uncle Neil, killed in a care home among thousands, with no inquiry or explanation

I remember his wit, his wisdom and his way with words

I remember Bosz, 52, the love of my life

I remember how much I love and miss you every single morning I wake without you Debs

I remember your smile, your touch, your smell, our walks, our talks, our laughter and tears, our kids, our life – now its tears, heartache, but filled with the laughter of our memories of you

I remember how Allan and myself could never decide what to do on our time together, he would say it was my turn to decide and I would say it was his, always got there in end

I remember how you loved our cruise holidays, how at the end of every night we would go out on the top deck, listen to the sea and look at the stars – it felt like it was only me and you on that ship, it felt like it was only you and me on the planet, now I just feel I am on the planet on my own

I remember the awful singing of the Balamory theme tune my dad Arthur sang and how I will never hear his voice again because of Covid. 💔🖤

I remember Jim being very particular in his appearance, house, car and lorry, which were always pristine – so much so he was nicknamed Big Gorgeous at work and asked if he wore his slippers in his cab due to how spotlessly clean it was

I remember not being able to visit Jim and hold his hand, tell him he was going to be OK, for the 35 days he was in hospital, and only able to talk to him via video call for the last 2 weeks of his life

I remember your joy and your eyes light up every time you seen Elijah

I remember Owen, bravest man, paraplegic poet, British judo champion

I remember Janice, fantastic, funny, caring nurse who will always be missed

I remember my lovely Dad who I miss every day

I remember my Mum, Jean, with love

I remember Margaret, a loving, caring wife, mum, nana and sister, love always from Adam, Mandy, Malcolm and family

I remember your infectious laugh, your Dunkirk spirit regarding everything healthwise you encountered – I remember YOU x


I remember our parents, Jim & Mary: you held our family together through the toughest of times – you fought so hard, for so long, and are so loved and missed by your daughters


I remember my Mum and Dad and the extra time that lockdown gave me to spend with them before their passing!


I remember Hazel, her infectious laugh and boundless energy


I remember Brian, rest in peace


I remember Alice always at the kitchen table


I remember my Linda with love and laughter 💕 x


I remember when I knew what happiness was because I met you – love you for a thousand years Lee


I remember your smile, Kim, as you talked about your wonderful boys and all their achievements

I remember Kathy, never forgotten, always close in our hearts

I remember my grandma, who died of sepsis but my family blamed the vaccine

I remember Ralph, agoraphobic for decades, rest his gentle soul – the carers didn't mean to bring Covid

I remember Jimmy, his zest for life, his love for his family and, most of all, the way he faced Covid with dignity and bravery

I remember scrambling for pennies at Uncle Malcolm's wedding all those years ago

I remember and miss John's infectious laugh – it brought tears to my eyes and thinking about it still does x

I remember my wife Linda who died on the 2nd February 2021 – memories of you I will always treasure in my heart, you will live forever ♥

I remember your hand squeezing mine, your laugh, your hugs, your advice, my dad

I remember when you lifted me on to your toes and waltzed me round a room

I remember feeling safe when you carried me on your shoulders

I remember as you grew old and your memory faded the stories might have been muddled but they were still so you

I remember everything – the bad singing, the Dad jokes and dancing, winding the kids up and how proud he was at all their achievements big or small and these are the wee moments I miss

I remember my Dad as my forever hero – Covid can't steal that

I remember Annie's adventures every week, always ending in coffee and something sweet

I remember my husband, Jamie, who just turned 32 the day before he went into hospital

I remember my beautiful, kind and caring sister Suzanne who was lost to Covid and who is loved and missed so very much

I remember my beautiful, vibrant, one of a kind best friend who took his own life during the 1st lockdown – love you forever Cindy!

I remember my beautiful care free, fun loving sister Agnes –
somewhere over the rainbow we'll be together again ♥


I remember playing with your hair, Maria, and stroking your face
as you fell asleep forever


I remember my mother Mary, who died in Covid times, but not of
Covid – I was lucky; I got to hold her at the end, just as she got
to hold me at my beginning


I remember Alex, devoted husband, father, grandfather and great-
grandfather – he would do anything for anyone, and died alone
and unacknowledged


I remember how full of fun you were, especially with your
grandsons, there was always laughter, always love – Covid took
you from us mum but it's not goodbye, it's only see you later


I remember the window that blocked us from holding you, and your
wave to say, *'I hear you'*, but mostly, Robert, I remember you, and
I will always love you


I remember how full of fun you were, especially with your grandsons,
there was always laughter, always love – Covid took you from
us mum, but it's not goodbye, it's only see you later

I remember you giving the best hugs, especially when I was wee and you were in your big mohair cardi'

I remember the laughter the day Jacky's false eye got stuck facing the wrong way!

I remember Aunt Rita's rendition of the Inverary Inn!

I remember when Covid took you from me, how I wish I had kept you safe 💔💔

I remember she scattered half of his ashes here, and half there, by the shore he loved

Acknowledgements

Scotland's Covid Memorial was commissioned by The Herald, who launched a campaign in association with bereaved families in Spring 2020, establishing a public fund, and accepting Glasgow City Council's offer of Pollok Country Park as a permanent home.

The installation in Pollok Country Park will include 40 wooden supports bearing the words 'I remember', along with QR-code linking to the audiobook, and memorial plantings of wildflowers. This book was published to coincide with the public opening of the first phase of the memorial, May 27, 2022.

Every 'I remember' was painted by the artist and buried at the memorial on March 14, 2022. A digital record will be deposited with National Library of Scotland. All contributions appear on the web-book: *iremember.scot/i-remember*

A selection of 'I remember' appears in an audiobook edited by Alec Finlay, read by Robert Carlyle, with sound design by Chris Watson, published on March 23, 2022. This is available to download free, with the option to donate to make a donation: *i-remember.bandcamp.com/releases*

Information on the memorial appears on The Herald's website: *heraldscotland.com/campaigns/i-remember*

The memorial was created with funds from private and public donors, including Scottish Government, Transport Scotland, Sir Tom Hunter, The Hunter Foundation, Lord Willie Haughey, City Charitable Trust, John Watson OBE, the Watson Foundation, Freemasons of Glasgow, Harry Clarke Group of Companies, and the generous donations of people across Scotland.

Scotland's Covid Memorial design concept: Alec Finlay
design collaborators: Ken Cockburn, Lucy Richards
artwork management: greenspace scotland
photography: Hannah Laycock
artwork maker: Alistair Letch
project assistant: Kate McAllan
landscape team: Glasgow City Council Parks and Leisure
jute ties: Fiona Moon
structural engineer: Lazlo Pitic
audiobook: Robert Carlyle
audiobook sound design: Chris Watson
archive: National Library of Scotland
publisher: Stewed Rhubarb

The artist wishes to thank: Covid-19 Families Scotland; Covid-19 Recovery Collective; Long Covid SOS; Long Covid Scotland; Covid Aid; Our Covid Stories; Columba 1400; Life Changes Trust; Paths for All; Marie Curie; the hidden gardens; Lapidus Scotland, NHS Scotland; Cruse Bereavement Care Scotland; Scottish Poetry Library; Stewed Rhubarb Press: Duncan Lockerbie & Charlie Roy; the Literary Agency; First Site (Colchester); with special thanks to Connie McCready, Peter McMahon, Carolyn Murdoch, Conor Walker, Michael MacLennan, Jenny Mason, Jenny O'Boyle, Kirsty White, Rachel Smith, Allison Greig, and Wayne Travis.

The Herald wishes to thank: Scotland's Covid Memorial steering and advisory panels, acknowledging the contribution of the late Ally McLaws; and National Trust Scotland.

List of contributors to the 'I remember' web-book, audiobook and book.

Liz Adams
Frances Ainslie
Vicky Allan
Angela Anderson
Deborah Anderson
Fiona Arnott-Barron
Morna Ball
Gabrielle Barnby
Joanne Barton
Meg Bateman
Heather Bath
Jackie Baxter
Henry Bell
Nicole Bell
Richard Berengarten
Ruth Bissell
Catriona Black
Angela Blacklock-Brown
Phoebe Boag
Dr Adam Boggon
Sharon Boswell
Alison Bowden
Felicity Bristow
Alison Brown
Moira Buckley
Lucy Bullimore
Rob Bushby
Larry Butler
Jack Butterworth

Colette Byrne
Patricia Cameron
Michelle Campbell
Robert Carlyle
John Cayley
Leonie Charlton
Lorna Christie
Christopher Maoilios Caimbeul
AC Clarke
Clair Clark
Paul Cleary
Ken Cockburn
Tamara Colchester
Jacqueline Collins
Mark Collins
David Connearn
Susan Connelly
Jane Cooper
Sheena Corcoran
William Cowan
Carlyn Coyle
Anna Craig
Fraser Cramond
Kevin Crowe
Moira Crumley
Lisa Davidson
Sandra Davison
Jamie Lee Dean

Tola Dehinde
Karen Dillon
Charmaine Dodds
Gwen Donald
Adele Donnelly
Michael Donnelly
Gillian Duff
Rebecca Edgerley
Sue Evans
Pauline Flanagan
Alec Finlay
Andrew Finlay
Clare Forrest
Linda France
Annette Fraser
Malcolm Fraser
Jane George
Ruth Gibson
John Glendy
Jan Gillan
Valerie Gillies
Diane Grainger
Gilllian Grant
Lorraine Grant
Allison Greig
Kelly Griffin
Mags Griffin
Sharon Gunason
Marlyn Guthrie
Alyson Hallett
Alan Halsey
Ian Hamilton
Seona Hamilton

Sarah Hardie
Suzanne Hargreaves
Rosaline Harkins
Caroline Harper
Anoushka Havinden
Kate Heaton
Gillian Heirs
Karen Herbison
Sue Hilder
Brian Hill
Lyra Hill
Andrew Hillhouse
Clare Hobba
Michelle Hunt
Janet Irvine
Mette Karlsvik
Janice Kerr
Alexandra Krause
Linda Kydd
Karen Lamb
Jane Lamb
Shirley Law
Laura Lawler
Meredith Leston
Garry Loftus
Kirsty Lear-Grant
Helen Lear-Grant
Stephanie Leca
Suze de Lee
Rod Leith
Caroline Lennon
Meredith Leston
Lindsay Pirrit

Gerry Loose
Andrea Lothian
Alasdair Macdonald
Joan MacDonald
Helen Mackenzie
Rebecca Mackie
Catherine MacLeod
Gary Maguire
Karen Malky
Jenny Mason
Adam Mathieson
Julie McAdam
Julie McAneny
Sheila Mcardles
Kathleen McCall
Natalie McCall
Connie McCready
Finlay McDermid
Marion McDonald
Theresa McGowan
Anne McHugh
Christine McInnes
Morven McKelvie
Jane Mckie
Bernadette McLaughlin
Ally Mclaws
Marianne McLeavey
Peter McMahon
Rosie McMillan
Hannah McNeilly
Lorraine McNerney
Jo Melvin
Carole Milligan

Leeanne Milne
Laura Moody
Helen Morrison
Jane Morrison
Jasper Morrison
Carolyn Murdoch
Lynn Murney
Grace Charteris Murray
Lisa Murray
Alice Neeve
Susan Nelis
Debbie Nelson
Scott Nelson
Katie Nicoll
Tracey Nimbley
Jenny O'Boyle
Kerry O'Connor
Cáit O'Neill McCullagh
Karen Park
Robin Park
Louise Parkes
Iain Pate
Hilary Paterson
Nadia Paterson
Jane Patience
Alison Patterson
Alistair Peebles
Emma Peters
Rhona Petrie
Chris Phillips
Anne Pollock
Margaret Porter
Marie Porter

Clare E Potter
Tom Pow
Pravdoliub Ivanov
Julie Procter
Conor Walker
Alison Riach
Lucy Richards
Craig Richardson
Kay Ritchie
Juliet Robertson
Agnes Rowland
Gill Russell
Stewart Sandison
Jackie Sands
Anasua Sarkaroy
Susan Scott
Carol Sellar
Catherine Shaw
Lynne Sherrie
Adam Smith
Chimére L Smith
Phil Smith
Lorna Borrowman Smith
Rachel Smith
Ann Traquair Smith
Holly Wren Spaulding
Heather Stewart
Leona Stewart
Elizabeth Stirling
Margaret Strick
Telfer Stokes
Dr Aaron Sutherland
Diana Sykes
Caroline Taylor
Sheila Templeton
Phillip Terry
Mary Thomson
Mhairi Thomson
Anne-Marie Tonner
Margaret Umeed
Jo Vergunst
Anne Watson
Gina Watson
Sharon Watson
Richard Watt
Johnathan Waugh
Debbie Whalen
Chris White
Kirsty White
Deborah Whitehorn
Mary Wight
Jayne Wilding
Alison Willacy
Christie Williamson
Paula Wilson
John Young

We continue to collect 'I remember'.
Email your contribution(s) to *iremember2021@yahoo.com*

The Herald: Scotland's Covid Memorial

Artist design concept: copyright Alec Finlay, ©2022
*'I remember'*, copyright of the Joe Brainard estate, ©1975, 2022
Design: Richy Lamb, with Alec Finlay
Print and binding: William Anderson and Sons, Glasgow

Published by Stewed Rhubarb in an edition of 750 copies, with a limited edition of 26 hardbound copies, signed and lettered by the artist

*iremember.scot*
*heraldscotland.com/campaigns/i-remember*
*alecfinlay.com*
*stewedrhubarb.org*

 £10.00